Wandering Woman: Oregon

The Ultimate Road Trip: One Woman's
Journey Across the United States by Car

Julie Bettendorf

Contents

Introduction

"Not all who wander are lost."

Are you sure? I thought to myself, as I tried not to panic. I was a long way from anything familiar, but that was how it should be. I had driven thousands of miles on dusty, pothole-filled roads. It's often on the worst roads that you can discover something truly amazing.

My dusty CRV was parked beside me, containing one restless dog and a variety of snack bags, all empty by now. There were no buildings in sight, no cars or people or movement at all. Only the constant humming of the insects as they buzzed around my head.

I turned to my left – another straight road that trailed off into the distance. I glanced over to the right, then behind me – two more barely discernible roads stretched out into the abyss. I was in a four-way intersection with no signs, no sense of direction, and no sign of life for several miles. No cell service either. *Damn*, I thought. *I'm lost*.

How did I get here? I couldn't help but feel like this little intersection was a cruel metaphor for life. I began to daydream, imagining each road might transport me back to a different time, a different role in my life, and a different me.

If I took the road from whence I came, it could lead me all the way back to Oregon, back to my cheating third husband, back to a life of loneliness and solitude. There is no greater loneliness than being married to someone who isn't actually present in your life.

If I took the road to my left, perhaps it could take me back to my career as a dental hygienist, a job I hated deep down in my soul. There is something so disengaging about cleaning teeth for a living. It's a disgusting, smelly way to get a paycheck. It pays well, which is great, but the best part is the huge gob of friends I enjoy to this day.

Or maybe the road to my right, *yes – maybe that's the path*, I imagined. Maybe it could take me back to my real treasure, my kids. Back to their smiling, innocent faces as toddlers, as they danced around the Christmas tree and their father and I were still married. Back when they still needed me for every little thing.

But, that was just it. I didn't feel needed anymore. My kids weren't toddlers anymore – they were both full-grown adults, and far too busy for me. My dental buddies were still working, but I wasn't. Dental hygiene had robbed me of the cartilage in my fingers, giving me severe, disabling arthritis. And, I wouldn't be returning to any more husbands either, because three marriages were quite enough for me.

All three of these paths, all three of these roles – the wife, the mother, and the dental hygienist – had seemingly been stripped from me within a year. I was lost and looking to find myself again.

The funny thing about this phrase, "not all who wander are lost" – is that, in my experience, wandering and being lost walk hand-in-hand with one another, and the expression can be flipped. In my experience, not all who are lost are wandering, and that is a real disservice to the beauty and clarity that the world has to offer.

When one becomes lost, wandering is the only option to guide oneself back to a path. After all, one could not come upon any dirt path at all without wandering.

I began wandering at an early age, both with my mind and with my feet. At eight years old, I was reading a book about archaeology and dreaming of one day seeing Egypt. I didn't follow a traditional path in high school either, going heavily into foreign languages, in hopes of one day using them.

At twenty-five years old, I divorced my first husband (the dental student who talked me into becoming a dental hygienist so I could work for him) and decided to give traveling a real shot. I took off for the Andes and Macchu Picchu, climbing up ancient Inca stone steps to reach the magnificent ruins.

Anyone who has been to Macchu Picchu will tell you there is something ethereal and deeply spiritual about the place. The ruins stretch out across the emerald green mountains, way up in the middle of the sky. Macchu Picchu gave me my first experience of feeling history. This trip inspired me to come back and complete a degree in archaeology, and I've been wandering ever since.

More travel followed including a backpack trip around Europe for three months, by myself, and trips to Britain, Italy, and Greece. I visited the burial places of Crusaders, mummies, and ancient kings. I happened upon the castle of my namesake in Bettendorf, Luxembourg, and wandered my way through European history.

My favorite excursion by far was finally seeing Egypt with my daughter in 2012. Just like my childhood dream envisioned, I rode a camel beneath the pyramids of Giza, with my head wrapped in some man's sweaty turban. It was perfect.

Traveling has always been my own personal antidote to pain. I went to Mexico after my first and second divorces, Canada after my third, and Italy after my dad died. Call it avoidance if you want, but I call it an accelerated form of healing in the purest sense of the word. I believe travel can heal your soul.

Wandering has always worked its wonders on me – made me feel renewed, rejoiceful, grateful, and purposeful. It's been my medicine.

So, as I stood in that intersection, I once again wondered how wandering had led me so astray this time. *What the hell am I supposed to do now?* It was then that I realized that one last path had not been considered yet – the path which stretched straight out in front of me. *Which role does this represent?* I pondered.

The answer smacked me in the face.

That last dirt road – the only path that could take me where I wanted to go, the only path that ever truly healed me or showed me the way – was the path of the traveler. The wife, the mother, and the hygienist roles – though valued in their time – were sitting in the bleachers now. It was time to welcome and enable my boldest, bravest, and perhaps most pivotal role yet:

The role of the Wandering Woman.

Welcome to Wandering Woman

This book is for you – the grieving empty nester mom, the begrudged housewife, the woman in need of a drastic change in her life. Really, this book is for anyone with a passion for traveling. If you feel lost with no sense of direction or purpose in life, that's a bonus – this book will be even more appealing to you. And lastly, if you're a man reading this book, congratulations for holding a book with the word woman in the title. You're contributing to gender equality, and that's pretty neat.

I decided to combine three of my dearest loves – travel, history, and archaeology – and put them into a book because I believe wandering has the power to change your life. I have been to many areas of the world and had too many outstanding experiences to list. However, by the time both my children had moved

Me

out in 2017, I had never seen my own country – America. It was the perfect time to explore a new country (my own) and discover a new me at the same time.

So, I packed up my Honda CRV, along with some gear and my 14-year-old furry friend, Sadie. Wandering Woman is the chronicle of my journey across eleven states, discovering the joy of getting lost and finding myself along the way.

Why America?

America, the beautiful? I sure think so, but I didn't realize just how beautiful our country is until I embarked on traveling across eleven western states in a year.

The United States offers everything for the discerning palate. From spectacular beaches, austere mountains, to rolling plains, our country has it all. It's difficult to comprehend just how large and impressive our scenery is, until you experience it first-hand, with the ultimate road trip.

I also realized just how much of our history is missing from U.S. history I was taught as a kid. The history of our country didn't begin with the pilgrims landing on Plymouth Rock in the 1600s. Our history is far more ancient, with rock art and archaeological sites dating back over 12,000 years.

We also owe a tremendous debt to early pioneers who tamed our land. The Mormons and other groups ventured into the great unknown with their families and their worldly possessions. Some of them pulled cumbersome handcarts across the country to settle in inhospitable, dangerous locations.

The goal of Wandering Woman is to bring history back to life and make it interesting again. I am presenting some famous sites, and many little-known ones. You will take the road-less-traveled with me, while we explore ghost towns, rock art sites, archaeological sites, and museums, to discover the colorful tapestry that is our country.

I present some history, including dates, but my goal is to present more of the real-life stories of history, including ghost stories, profiles in history, voices from the past, and moments in time, to give you, the reader, a deeper understanding of the context of history.

This is by no means an exhaustive list of places to visit. In fact, I encourage you to discover America for yourself, as I did, by making a trek across the land by car. You can explore as the early explorers did, just a little more comfortably, with a lot less hardship.

I hope you enjoy this book and take a little time out to discover our beautiful country, and maybe even discover yourself in the process.

Safe Travels,

Julie Bettendorf

Welcome to Oregon

The Beaver State

*O**regon** is my home state. It's a gorgeous, green place, in part thanks to copious amounts of rain. The green is also thanks to the values of Oregonians to honor the environment and take care of what is entrusted to them. Oregon is a comfortable state, where you can kick off your shoes and stay awhile.

5 things to love about Oregon:

- Fantastic coastal scenery like Cape San Sebastian

- The spectacular scenery of the Columbia River Gorge

- Oregon Trail history in places like Baker City

- Early maritime history in places like Astoria

- Lewis & Clark history in places like Fort Clatsop

Dreams of Oregon

"Portland, Oregon won't build a mile of road without a mile of bike path. You can commute there, even with that weather, all the time." – **Lance Armstrong**

"I think everyone born in Oregon is an environmentalist by birth."– **Ted Knight**

"Oregon is an inspiration. Whether you come to it, or are born to it, you become entranced by our state's beauty, the opportunity she affords, and the independent spirit of her citizens." – **Tom McCall**

Top Stuff to See in Oregon

Favorite Oregon Historical Sites:

- Pendleton Underground
- Jacksonville

Favorite Oregon Ghost Towns:

- Golden
- Shaniko

Favorite Oregon Museums:

- Pioneer Museum, Brownsville
- Baker Heritage Museum, Baker City

Favorite Oregon Scenic Drives:

- Highway 101, down the Oregon Coast

- Wallowa-Whitman National Forest, along Highway 7

When driving through Oregon, be on the lookout for:

Elk and deer, sometimes in the middle of the road

Early Oregon

Early Hot Lake Springs

Early Dalles Residents

Courtesy of Oregon Trail Interpretive Center

Northwestern Oregon

Fort Stevens

Astoria

A **storia** was the first American colony to be established on
the coast of North America. It offers a commanding view
of where the Columbia River meets the Pacific Ocean, and you

can easily observe barges and large vessels as they make their way along. The town of Astoria is a charming place, full of old buildings and great seafood.

When you are in Astoria, a must-see is the remarkable *Flavel House*. Built in 1886, this Queen Anne style mansion was the home of Captain George Flavel, an early pilot boat captain in Astoria.

The house has many of the original furnishings owned by the Flavel family.

The Flavel House also boasts six magnificent fireplaces, each with imported tiles from around the world.

The house is 11,600 square feet of luxury, complete with a four story tower and metal bathtubs.

Fort Astoria, which was begun in 1811, was a cornerstone of the massive fur trading empire envisioned by John Jacob Astor. The first white woman settler to live in the Oregon Country settled here in 1814. She was an English barmaid named Jane Barnes.
Finch

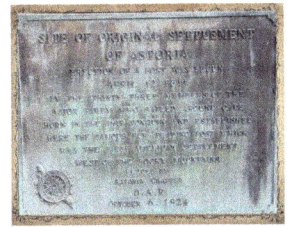

All that remains of the fort today is this reconstructed guard tower.

The ***Columbia River Maritime Museum*** is another must-see while in Astoria. The museum covers early maritime history including Coast Guard service, and one of my favorite topics—shipwrecks.

From the earliest days of sailing ships, the Columbia River Bar has long been a hazard. In 1846, the USS Shark, wrecked there.

An inscribed stone was found near where the ship had wrecked. It reads *"The Shark was lost Sept. 10, 1846."*

Artifacts from the ship are featured in the museum, including an officer's sword, still encrusted from its time in the sea.

Some of my favorite pieces are blue and white porcelain, brought back from China in 1792, by Captain Robert Gray, an early seafaring explorer to the Northwest.

How to get to Astoria Historical Sites:

- The Flavel House is located at 714 Exchange St, Astoria.

- The remains of Fort Astoria are located at 1498 Exchange St, Astoria.

- The Columbia River Maritime Museum address is 1792 Marine Dr, Astoria.

A word about early settlement in the Northwest:

The initial creation of a fur trading empire by John Jacob Astor resulted in the deaths of 61 people out of a total of about 140, from drowning on the Columbia Bar, Indian attacks, destruction of ships, and illness and injury.

The Overland Party, one of the two explorations to Astoria, discovered the first route which could be used by wagons to cross the country. They discovered the route through South Pass to cross the Rockies in Wyoming. This same route was later used by settlers crossing the Oregon Trail. [Stark]

In the 1840s, settlers kept going further west, making their way to the Willamette Valley. Elderly Marie Dorion was already living there.

Profiles in history:

Marie Dorion was a Native American woman who was part of Hunt's overland party to set up Astoria. Marie was married to Pierre Dorion, the interpreter. She traveled across the country while pregnant and caring for her two and five year-old children. She gave birth to a third child while traveling through Baker Valley, Oregon, and rested only about one day before rejoining the Overland Party traveling west.

The small infant lived only a week. Her husband Pierre and several others were killed by Indians near the Snake River. Marie fled with her children on horseback. It was January, with snow so deep she couldn't travel further, so she camped in a ravine. She killed two horses, smoked the horsemeat, and used the hides to create a shelter. It was here she stayed until March. Stark

She eventually settled in the Willamette Valley in Oregon and was already well established when the first settlers arrived in Oregon in the 1840s. She died in 1850, being revered as an "extraordinary

woman, the oldest in the neighborhood, kindly, patient, and de-vout." [Stark]

John Jacob Astor was born in Walldorf, Germany. His father wanted John Jacob to help him run his butcher shop, but John Jacob had other ideas. In March 1784, he arrived in Chesapeake Bay at the age of 21. On board ship, he met a fur trader who started John Jacob thinking about building a vast fur trading empire.

In the mid 1780s, he set up in Manhattan, selling exotic fur pelts and fine European musical instruments, to cater to the refined tastes of New Yorkers. In 1808, Astor wrote a letter of introduction, telling President Thomas Jefferson of his plans to create a fur trading empire on the West Coast, and the plans for Astoria began. John Jacob Astor died in 1848 at the age of 84. He became the richest man in the United States, worth about 20 million dollars, or 110 billion in today's dollars. He ranks fourth in the list of all-time wealthiest Americans. [Stark]

Voices from the past:

"Your name will be handed down with that of Columbus & Raleigh, as the father of the establishment and the founder of such an empire." ***Thomas Jefferson to John Jacob Astor*** [Stark]

"There were 1200 people on the Great Republic, which was wrecked on the Columbia River bar in 1875. Everyone was taken off in lifeboats to Astoria, and escaped for their lives, except 14 people in the last lifeboat which capsized and drowned its occupants." **John Bentley, carpenter, on losing his machinery, but not his life, on the Great Republic shipwreck.**

A moment in time:

The ***Tonquin*** dropped anchor off the Northwest Coast and the mouth of the Columbia River on March 22, 1811, after sailing 21,852 miles. The captain of the Tonquin, Jonathan Thorn, was a forceful, authoritarian commander who was responsible for the deaths of at least 8 people. He had sent them out in small boats to locate a passage over the bar. Previous to the Tonquin, only about 20 ships had succeeded in crossing the Columbia Bar.

After unloading supplies, materials, and trade goods, Captain Thorn sailed further north to trade with the Clayoquot Indians of British Columbia. Negotiations didn't go well and the Clayoquot, who had climbed aboard the ship, left angrily. The Clayoquot came back a few days later, this time with more Indians. The Tonquin was teeming with Clayoquot. At a signal from a Clayoquot Chief, the warriors began clubbing the crew to death. The third man to die was Captain Thorn.

Five men aboard the Tonquin survived. Four of the five chose to take the longboat and make for Astoria, 200 miles south. The fifth man stayed aboard the Tonquin. The Clayoquot, thinking all was safe with only one man on board, climbed aboard the Tonquin in large numbers. What they didn't count on was that the fifth man would light the entire nine thousand pounds of powder onboard the Tonquin, blowing the ship, himself, and the hundreds of Clayoquot who had climbed aboard, to bits. The four men who left in the longboat were soon captured and tortured to death by the remaining Clayoquot. Stark

The 1000 pound anchor of the Tonquin was found by a crab fisherman just off Vancouver Island in 2003. The anchor was crusted over with blue glass beads, a common trading item for John Jacob Astor's empire in Astoria. Stark

Ghost story:

The Flavel House has several ghosts and visitors have heard voices, and music playing. The music is thought to be the ghost of Nellie Flavel, who was a classically trained pianist.

A female ghost has been seen on the second floor, and Captain Flavel himself has been seen in his bedroom. Captain Flavel died in the bedroom in 1893. Kitmacher

Fort Clatsop

F*ort Clatsop* was the winter quarters of the Lewis and Clark Expedition from 1805-1806. By the time Lewis & Clark arrived in what would be Fort Clatsop, they had already traveled over 4000 miles. They arrived into the area and began to build Fort Clatsop on December 10, 1805.

They spent Christmas and the next three months at Fort Clatsop, leaving the fort on March 23, 1806. The explorers recorded that it rained almost every one of the 106 days the group spent there. Only 12 days were without precipitation. NPS

They suffered from flea infestation, colds, flu, rheumatic pain, and other hardships. A common complaint was the presence of mosquitoes.

A small group journeyed to what is now Seaside, Oregon to process salt from sea water. In what is now Cannon Beach, a group of Tillamook Indians processed a dead whale which had washed up to shore. They shared some of the blubber with the explorers. The corps mem-

bers compared the blubber to
the flavor of dog or beaver. [Jones]

How to get to Fort Clatsop:

Fort Clatsop is located near Astoria at 92345 Fort Clatsop Road.

A word about Lewis & Clark's Corp of Discovery:

In 1803, President Thomas Jefferson funded the expedition with
$2500. The group was to find the most direct water route to the
Pacific. Meriwether Lewis, who was a family friend of Jefferson
was put in charge of the expedition. He enlisted his friend from
the Indian campaigns, William Clark.

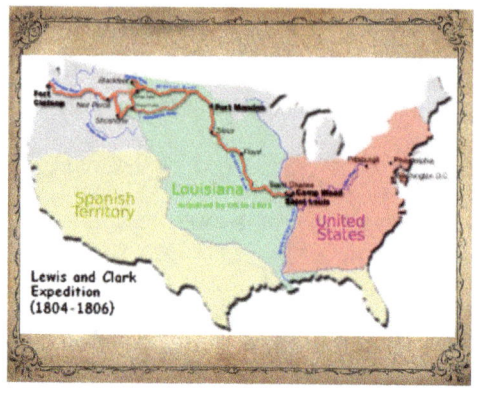

Meriwether Lewis and his men left Pittsburgh on August 31, 1803. They stopped in Clarksville, Indiana to pick up William Clark and additional men. The group left St. Louis, Missouri on May 15, 1804. When they left, Clark was 33, and Lewis was 29.

They spent their first winter among the Mandan tribe in North Dakota, establishing Fort Mandan. It was here that they added French explorer Charbonneau and his wife Sacajawea. They left Fort Mandan in April of 1805, heading up the Missouri River. They reached the Pacific Ocean in November of 1805. The journey would eventually take 28 months and the group would travel 8000 miles. [Jones]

Fun facts:

- Clark paid his interpreter Charbonneau a total of $500 and 33 and 1/3 cents for his services on the expedition.

- There is a myth among the Nez Perce that the sister of Chief Red Grizzly Bear had a son with Clark. The boy had light hair and often proclaimed "Me Clark."

- Venereal disease was common among the Indians they met. A few of the party suffered the effects from encounters with the women. Gonorrhea was a frequent problem, and what Lewis called Louis Venerae.

- Sacajawea was promised to another Indian man, but because she had a child with Charbonneau, the Indian didn't want her. During the expedition, Charbonneau hit Sacajawea and was reprimanded by Clark.

- Early in the expedition, several men were court-martialed and whipped for "having uttered repeated expressions of a highly criminal and mutinous nature," and desertion.

- Clark suffered from foot problems, and Lewis suffered from depression.

- During the expedition, the group endured hunger, disease,

subzero temperatures, blizzards, fierce rapids, grizzly bear attacks, thick clouds of mosquitoes, and repeated robberies by Indians. They also were reduced to eating their dogs and colts to stay alive.

- They wrote nearly one million published words in journals of their trip.

- Only 1 out of 9 practicing doctors actually had a medical degree in Lewis & Clark's time. Most were trained on-the-job, including Lewis and Clark.

- Medications they took along including a variety of potent laxatives known as "Thunderclappers." They also brought along penile syringes to treat venereal disease by injecting a solution into the urethra.

- Lancets were purchased for "therapeutic" bloodletting. Opium and a 10% opium solution known as Laudanum were used quite frequently on the trip. An ointment made of ground beetles was used to create blisters, believed to act as a "counterirritant" Lead acetate was used in "eye-washes" which were traded with Columbia Basin Indians. The total cost of all medical supplies was $90.60. [Peck]

Profiles in history:

William Clark was born August 1, 1770 in Virginia. He was a friendly, extroverted person. After the Lewis and Clark Expedition, Clark became superintendent of Indian affairs in the Louisiana Territory, becoming Governor of Missouri territory in 1810. He died in St. Louis on Sept. 1, 1838, at the age of 68. [Peck]

Meriwether Lewis was born August 18, 1774. Lewis was a well-educated aristocrat. He became part of the Chosen Rifle Company where he met William Clark. Lewis was expedition leader and asked Clark to join him on the venture. Lewis died in October, 1809, suddenly and violently at an inn where he was staying. There is controversy over whether he was murdered or committed suicide. He suffered from depression and consumed alcohol and opium. He was 35. [Peck]

York was born in 1770 and was William Clark's African American slave. He was responsible for carrying provisions, hunting game, gathering water and performing other tasks for Clark. York was occasionally ordered to dance, which "amused the crowd very much." York was sometimes paraded in front of Native Americans, who marveled at his muscular body and called him "big medicine." After the expedition, York requested to be freed, but Clark refused. He remained a slave until at least 1816, and died of cholera in 1832. [Strahn]

Sacajawea was born in Idaho around 1788, a member of the Lemhi Shoshone tribe. She was captured by Hidatsa when she was 12, and one year later, she was sold into marriage with Toussaint Charbonneau, a French-Canadian trapper.

They lived among the Mandan in North Dakota. Sacajawea was pregnant and only 16 years old when she joined the Lewis and Clark Expedition as a guide and interpreter.

Sacajawea was responsible for saving the journals of Lewis and Clark, when the records fell into the river. According to Native American oral traditions, Sacajawea died in 1884 and is buried in Wyoming.

Fort Stevens

Fort Stevens is a massive military compound, built in 1863, during the Civil War. The fort is named for General Isaac Stevens, governor of the Washington Territory.

The fort was meant to protect the Columbia River against invasion from Canada by the British. It was believed the British might side with the Confederates during the Civil War.

The earthworks were built first, and consist of a ditch and huge mounds of earth, on top of which are cannon.

In 1897, concrete batteries and large guns were added.

Fort Stevens was in use during wars with Native Americans, the Civil War, Spanish-American War, and both World Wars.

Today, as you walk around Fort Stevens, you can see several buildings, including the **brick guardhouse**, and the **power station**, and an interesting shell of a building, known as the **plotting room.**

Fort Stevens was shelled by a Japanese submarine on June 21, 1942, marking the only time and place the contiguous United States mainland was attacked during World War II.

On the beach at Fort Stevens, you can also see what's left of the *Peter Iredale*, a steel sailing vessel which wrecked there on October 25, 1906.

How to get to Fort Stevens:

Fort Stevens is located near Hammond, Oregon, about 9 miles south of Astoria.

Ghost story:

Visitors to Fort Stevens report seeing figures of soldiers in full battle gear, one carrying a flashlight, and another carrying a knife. Two ghosts have been seen in Civil War uniforms. Voices and footsteps have also been heard. Kitmacher

A word about the Neahkahnie Mountain Treasure:

Further south along the Oregon coast, off Hwy 101 and on the shores of Nehalem Bay, there is a mountain named Neahkahnie, which is a Chinook word meaning "home of the fire god." An old legend survives about this mountain, handed down through generations of Native Americans, and finally passed on to white explorers and settlers.

It tells of a Spanish ship in the bay in the late 1600s. The ship is believed to be the Santo Cristo de Burgos, wrecked in 1693. Several Spaniards rowed ashore and walked inland and up the mountain, carrying a chest.

They eventually stopped and buried the chest, with the natives watching the event. The Spaniards then proceeded to stab a dark-skinned man who was with them, and bury the poor man with the chest. This was apparently to keep the natives from disturbing the treasure.

One hundred years later, white explorers arrived. The natives shared tales of the treasure with the explorers. Thus began the exploration and pillaging of Neahkahnie Mountain. In the 1870's, a treasure hunter discovered stones marked with letters, arrows, and crosses. Blocks of beeswax have also been found

on the mountain. They are believed to be from the ship, because beeswax was shipped by the Spanish for use in Catholic masses.

There is a rumor that the treasure was found back in the early 1800's by a Hudson's Bay Company fur trapper who spent time digging on the mountain. The man left suddenly, quitting his job with the Hudson's Bay Company, and settling at French Prairie on the Willamette. The man seemed to suddenly have plenty of money in a time where others were still using wheat to pay for things.

Fort Yamhill

Fort Yamhill was built in 1856, the same year Oregon became a state. Unlike other forts, Fort Yamhill was built to protect the Native Americans from hostile settlers.

The fort served as prevention against violence, and was not meant to engage in battle. The fort was held by regular army from 1856-1861.

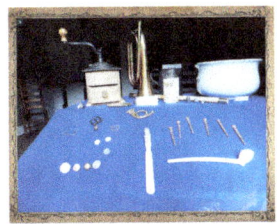

Several Civil War generals from both the Union and Confederate armies served at Fort Yamhill. The fort was also once commanded by General Philip Sheridan.

Not much remains of the original fort, but there are numerous historical placards to give you a sense of where the buildings stood.

Fort Yamhill had 24 buildings including a Sutler's store, officer's quarters, bakehouse, blacksmith shop, hospital, and mess room.

Only 2 buildings still stand, the original *officer's quarters*, and the *blockhouse*, which has been moved to nearby Grande Ronde.

How to get to Fort Yamhill:

Fort Yamhill is located off of Hwy. 18 near Grande Ronde.

Voices from the past:

"The threatening attitude of the community led me to apprehend a general and combined attack upon the camp of friendly Indians, located at the Grande Ronde, and the slaughtering or driving into hostile position all who might be residing in the valley." **Letter from Joel Palmer, Superintendent of Indian Affairs in Oregon, to the Commissioner of Indian Affairs, April 11, 1856.**

"Snow, hails, and rains alternately. Strange and rapid changes in the weather take place here every day. Some Indians steal a few potatoes from the Agency root-houses last night. Poor devils are starving." **from a soldier's journal at Fort Yamhill, March 26, 1864.**

Portland

Portland is the quintessential big city with a small town feel. Portlanders are proud of being a Portlander. When you visit Portland, you will discover why. The city has charming neighborhoods like the Pearl District and Hawthorne District, and countless casual coffee houses, along with high-end culture.

When you visit Portland, make a stop at the ***Oregon Historical Society*** and gaze at the many historical photos and artifacts of logging life, and spectacular wilderness back in the day.

The top floor of the museum contains older artifacts relating to Oregon history. Finch

Also take a trip through the past by taking the ***Portland Underground Tour.*** You will stroll through tunnels used to shanghai men into "white slavery" which existed from 1850 through 1941.

Just outside of Portland, in Oregon City, the **McLoughlin House** makes for a fascinating stop. The house was the residence of John McLoughlin and dates from 1846, complete with antiques and period furnishings. In 1909, efforts were made to save the house from demolition and turn the building into a museum.

How to get to Portland:

Portland is located in Northwestern Oregon, about 3 hours south of Seattle, Washington.

Profiles in history:

John McLoughlin was born in 1784 in Quebec, Canada. He was famous for being superintendent of the Hudson's Bay Company, helping to supply provisions for thousands of emigrants traveling the Oregon Trail. He would often let settlers buy provisions on credit, which resulted in him losing his job with the Hudson's Bay Company.

After the job loss, he decided to make a home for himself and his wife in Oregon City, so he built the mansion, now known as the McLoughlin House, in 1846. He also established Fort Vancouver in Washington in 1825 and Oregon City in 1842. Dr. John McLoughlin died in 1857, and is sometimes known as the "Father of Oregon." [Hill]

Ghost story:

The bodies of McLoughlin and his wife were moved from their original burial site to a site on the McLoughlin House property, and the hauntings began. Ghostly apparitions have been seen, along with hearing footsteps on the stairs, and a harpsichord playing. A rocking chair in McLoughlin's room also has been seen to rock on its own. Marguerite, his wife, has been seen looking out of the second story window. [Weeks]

There have been tales of ghosts in Portland's Underground. One such tale is that of crewmembers being shanghaied onto a ship named the Jennifer Jo. The men were viciously beaten and drugged before being loaded onto the ship and chained below deck. The ship left Portland with the shanghaied men, but the ship later sank in the Columbia River. The men below decks, still chained, drowned. Reports of being touched by wet hands, screaming, and moaning have been experienced in Portland's Underground. Some say it is the shanghaied men returned from the Jennifer Jo.
Kitmacher

Brownsville

Brownsville is a lovely little town that was founded in 1846 and is one of Oregon's first settlements. Pioneer families named Kirk, Brown, and Blakely, came west on the Oregon Trail and settled here.

There is a **statue** of the brown family in a prominent place on the street.

As you stroll along the streets in Brownsville, look out for the many historic buildings from the 1800s, including the **Moyer House**, built in 1881.

Other buildings include the *C.J. Howe Building*, built in 1908, the *Starr + Blakely Drugstore*, built in 1875, and the *Masonic Lodge*, built in 1865.

The *Pioneer Museum*, housed in the *Southern Pacific Railroad Depot* built in 1895, is a fantastic place to spend a few hours.

They have many artifacts that came over on the Oregon Trail, including the Drinkard Wagon from 1865. It's one of only three wagons left which has made the trek across the Oregon Trail.

There are complete rooms full of period pieces, including a doctor's office from the early 1900's, and a great selection of books and gifts.

Brownsville was also the site of much of the "Stand by Me" movie. The movie is commemorated every year during "Stand by Me Days." Town of Brownsville

How to get to Brownsville:

Brownsville is just a few miles off of Interstate 5, about 60 miles south of Portland.

Western Oregon

Heceta Head

Heceta Head Lighthouse

The ***Heceta Head Lighthouse***, located near Florence, Oregon, was built in 1893. It was the most expensive lighthouse to build on the Oregon Coast. The land was named for the Spanish explorer Bruno de Heceta who explored the coast during the late 1700s.

How to get to Heceta Head Lighthouse:

Heceta Head is located near Florence, Oregon at 725 Summer Street.

Ghost story:

Over 100 years ago, a young girl drowned near Heceta Head and is buried somewhere on the grounds of the lighthouse. Her mother, saddened by the death of her daughter, killed herself.

The mother, known as the Lady in Gray, now haunts the lighthouse. She is said to have cleaned up broken window glass left by a frightened maintenance man. Weeks

There is another ghost story about a lighthouse. This one centers around Yaquina Head Lighthouse, built in 1873 near Newport. The lighthouse has both inner and outer walls.

During construction, as workers filled in the space between the walls with rubble, a construction worker fell in between the walls. They couldn't get his body out, so the man was forever entombed in the lighthouse. Occasional hammering against the walls has been heard by visitors.

A moment in time:

On January 26, 1700, a massive wave hit the Oregon Coast. The *Great Tsunami of 1700* was caused by a magnitude 9 earthquake occurring in the Cascadia Subduction Zone, which runs from northern California to British Columbia.

The earthquake caused the ocean floor to move up 20 feet, resulting in the massive 50-foot wave forming. The tsunami hit the shoreline in about 20 minutes, flattening the area around Siletz Bay and destroying many Native American Villages. The Native Americans have preserved this event in their oral traditions.

Central Oregon

John Day Fossil Beds

Shaniko

Shaniko began its life in 1874 as a rail station and post office run by a German fellow named Scherneckau, which the local Native Americans pronounced "Shaniko."

Many of the buildings, including the *schoolhouse*, date to the early 1900s. Weis

Shaniko has all the ambience of a ghost town, and as you walk around, you will see a few historic buildings, and a few historic vehicles too.

How to get to Shaniko:

Shaniko is located in Central Oregon off of Oregon Route 218.

Peter Skene Ogden Bridge

T he ***Peter Skene Ogden Bridge*** is now a rest stop on Hwy. 97 in Central Oregon, near the town of Redmond.

I have passed it by so many times while traveling down the highway. Take a rest and walk along to admire the bridge and the history behind it.

Peter Skene Ogden came through here in 1825, as part of the first recorded journey into Central Oregon.

How to get to Peter Skene Ogden Bridge:

The Peter Skene Ogden Bridge is located in Central Oregon, off of Hwy 97, near the town of Terrebonne.

Profiles in history:

Peter Skene Ogden was born in 1790 in Quebec City. He gained success as a fur trapper, trader, and explorer. He was said to have a bullying nature, and in 1818, he was suspected in the death of an Indian trapper, which tarnished his reputation and sent him west.

He discovered Mount Shasta, traveling all over the West in search of fur. He also rescued the survivors of the Whitman Massacre. Ogden, Utah was named after him. He died in 1854 in Oregon City, Oregon.

Fort Rock

Fort Rock is one of the oldest archaeological sites in North America. Carbon dating dates it back over 13,000 years ago. It began as a large island in the middle of an ice-age lake.

Water slowly hollowed out the inside to form the crescent shape of today's Fort Rock.

I took a great little hike inside the Rock. It's a beautiful, desolate spot.

Not far away is Fort Rock Cave. It's on private property so you can't go there, but back a few decades ago, over 70 sandals were found in a heap. The sandals are over 9000 years old.

How to get to Fort Rock:

Fort Rock is located in Central Oregon, off of County Road 5-11A.

John Day Fossil Beds

When you visit the *John Day Fossil Beds*, the real star is the scenery. The hills are painted in various shades of green, red, and orange.

The road meanders through narrow little passageways, carved by time. There are three separate areas; *Sheep Rock*, *Clarno*, and *Painted Hills*.

There are several areas of the fossil beds to explore, with some excellent hikes.

The *Sheep Rock Unit* has a *Visitor's Center* with fossil exhibits, including the skulls of a "marsh rhino" and the "John Day tiger."

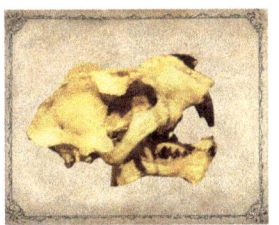

Plant and mammal fossils date from 45 million to 5 million years ago. Finch

How to get to John Day Fossil Beds:

The John Day Fossil Beds are located in East-Central Oregon, near the town of John Day.

Profiles in history:

John Day was originally from Virginia and served as a hunter with the Hunt Overland Party to help establish Astoria. He became very ill and temporarily lost his mind due to tragedy and hardship he endured while a member of the party.

He had been stripped naked by Indians near "the Narrows" (what is now the Dalles) and left to wander without food or water. He attempted suicide by taking two guns and shooting himself in the head. Amazingly, he survived the attempt. [Stark]

He later went to work for the rival North West Company as a hunter. He died in 1819 or 1820 near Little Lost River, Idaho and is immortalized by the town of John Day, Oregon and the John Day River. [Stark]

Voices from the past:

"Day was tall with a "handsome, open, manly countenance." At 40 years old, he was "a prime woodsman, and an almost unerring shot" with "an elastic step as if he trod on springs."" — ***Washington Irving, author***

Northeastern Oregon

Columbia River Gorge Near the Dalles

The Dalles

*T**he Dalles** has a lot of history, which you can learn more about in the **Fort Dalles Museum**.*

It's a wonderful place, housed in the army surgeon's quarters, built in 1856. The building itself is beautiful and it's full of artifacts about early pioneer and military life.

There are entire rooms filled with period furniture, including some fantastically ornate Oriental pieces.

The museum has an extensive collection of artifacts, including a handmade hunting knife found on the Oregon Trail.

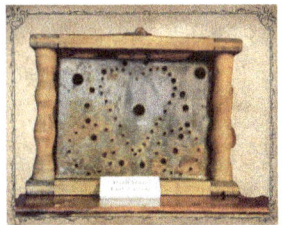

One of my favorite pieces is a handmade foot warmer.

On the grounds is another building containing marvelous old vehicles including The Umatilla House Omnibus from 1879.

Fort Dalles was established in 1850 as Fort Dunn, and became Fort Dalles in 1855. The fort's main function was to protect emigrants traveling along the Oregon Trail. Fort Dalles was abandoned in 1867. [Hill]

You should also visit the ***Columbia Gorge Discovery Center,*** in a wonderful location next to the Columbia River. When I visited, it was a bright, sunny day and the beauty of the golden grass against the dark blue water was absolutely spectacular.

It's a great museum with some interesting items, including some early school artifacts, and early camera equipment. Native American artifacts include a petroglyph dating from 1400 AD to 1600 AD, recovered from the Celilo Falls area, and basketry.

Columbia Gorge Discovery Center

The grounds make for an enjoyable short walk. There are various historic buildings and cabins, along with wagons, and old farming machinery.

How to get to Fort Dalles Museum and Columbia Gorge Discovery Center:

Both areas are in the Dalles, which is located off of I-84, along the Columbia River. The Fort Dalles Museum is located at 500 W. 15th and Garrison Streets. The Columbia Gorge Discovery Center is located at 5000 Discovery Drive.

Pendleton

P *endleton* is a nice town which looks like it is straight out of
the old west, which it is.

I took the **Pendleton Under-ground Tour** while I was there. It had been on my bucket list for a long time. The tour didn't disappoint.

You start out in the **Shamrock Card Room**, and pay a visit to **Hop Sing's Chinese laundry.**

Underneath the earth, you will stroll through the **meat market**, **ice cream parlor**, an **opium den**, a **speak easy** from prohibition days, and a **brothel**. A lot happened underground apparently. [Finch]

How to get to Pendleton:

Pendleton is located in Northeastern Oregon, just off Interstate 84.

Voices from the past:

"One time, during a diphtheria epidemic, I worked all night making five caskets for the children of Mr. and Mrs. Ben Ogle. The five of them died of this disease and were buried on the same day. My wife held the light for me that night as I made those coffins, and it was morning before I finally completed them." John Bentley, carpenter, on what it was like to serve as undertaker in early Pendleton.

Eastern Oregon

Spectacular Eastern Oregon

Hot Lake Springs

H**ot Lake* is one of the oldest areas of European settlement in the Northwest. The ***Hot Lake Springs Hotel was built in 1864 and the grounds contain the massive ***hotel building***, an 1812 ***trading post,*** and a replica of an 1800s ***chapel***.

The men of the William Price Hunt expedition came to the Hot Lake Springs area on New Year's Day in 1812.

Fur traders began to use the hot springs, as did thousands of Oregon Trail pioneers.

The hotel was built by two pioneers and once housed a blacksmith's shop, post office, barber shop, drug store, dance hall, garden shop and bath houses.

In 1917, the hotel became a hospital and sanitorium, and was known as the "Mayo Clinic of the West" The Mayo brothers were frequent guests at Hot Lake. Hot Lake Hotel

The most fascinating section for me was the third floor of the hotel which houses medical equipment and rooms from when the hotel served as a sanitorium.

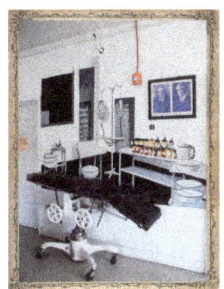

How to get to Hot Lake:

Hot Lake is located in Eastern Oregon, about 10 miles east of LaGrande.

Oregon Trail Interpretive Park

A t the ***Oregon Trail Interpretive Park***, the surroundings are beautiful, and the evidence of the Oregon Trail is poignant.

This route was used from the late 1830s through 1860s to forge a way into the Willamette Valley. The route was already well-established when it was used by hopeful prospectors looking for gold in 1861. Wallowa Whitman National Forest

Numerous signs mark different portions of this trail, and you can see wagon ruts and an old stagecoach trail.

There is also a wonderful reconstructed wagon, pioneer trunk,
and reconstructed pioneer grave
at the site.

How to get to Oregon Trail Interpretive Park:

Take exit 248 off I-84 near LaGrande, Oregon.

A word about the Oregon Trail:

The Oregon Trail travels across
six states beginning with Missouri, then Kansas, Nebraska,
Wyoming, Idaho, and finally,
Oregon. Different branches of
the Oregon Trail were used by
groups of emigrants, and came to
be known as the California Trail
and the Mormon Trail. The entire route was also known as the
Overland Trail. Glassman

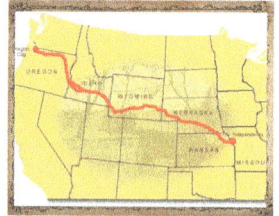

Between the years 1840 and 1866, approximately 500,000 pioneers traveled west on the trail. People died from diseases like scurvy, dysentery, and malaria. Many simply starved. Others suffered gunshot wounds.

It is believed that 34,000 to 45,000 people died along the trail, an average of between 17 and 22 lives per mile. Of the dead, only about 200 grave locations are known, most of which are unmarked. Many were intentionally buried in the path of the wagons, so any signs of a grave would not be noticed. Only about 20% of the Oregon Trail Ruts are identifiable today. [Wagner]

Voices from the past:

"Just threw my mirror way some while back. Why I couldn't bear the sight of my face no more, all over with creases and splotches. Looking so...so common. But my feet. Well, there is no escaping the sight of my feet. I watch them step after step, mile after mile. Won't fit no proper shoes." **Unknown Oregon Trail Pioneer.**

"Honore Liberty Timfret, wife of Zabel Timfret, I am. Birthed four fine girls and a son, I did. But that's forever been taken from me. My Timothy and Elizabeth fell to cholera early on. Somehow my heart hardened to sustain me. It took me quite a spell, you can imagine, but most recently the sight of graves has gone almost unnoticed. I begged Zabel for some kind of marker to show my child's spot. "How will Jesus find them without a marker" But no amount of cajolin' or cryin' would change that man's mind. So, we buried them back there in the great nothing with nary a thing to mark the spot but the never-ending wind." **Honore Timfret, Oregon Trail Pioneer.**

Baker City

B *aker City* is a picturesque city in Eastern Oregon. It was a prominent destination along the Oregon Trail.

In fact, the **Oregon Trail Interpretive Center** can be found there. The center has some fascinating historical photographs and Oregon Trail artifacts.

One of my favorite pieces is a delicate porcelain doll, a prized possession carried by a young pioneer back in the day. Oregon Trail Interpretive Center

Off the main highway, you can also see original ruts from the Oregon Trail wagons.

While I was in Baker City, I went to the ***Baker Heritage Museum***, a fascinating collection of antiques including wagons, musical instruments, furnishings, and just about everything you could think of.

The movie "Paint Your Wagon" was filmed in Baker City, so there were a lot of props and information from the movie.

Don't miss the upstairs, where there are full rooms of furnishings from the past, including an optometry office, a medical office, complete with a very scary X-ray machine and a barber shop with an equally frightening hair curling device. Baker Heritage Museum

How to get to Baker City:

Baker City is located in Eastern Oregon off Route 86.

Profiles in history:

Ezra Meeker took his first trip over the Oregon Trail when he was 22 years old, and his last trip was a fly-over when he was 94. Ezra left Indiana in 1852, with his wife Eliza, their 7 week old son, and Ezra's brother. They wished to join the wagons headed west to Oregon. The trip to Portland would take the group 5 months.

Ezra lost 20 pounds by the end of the trip, and had to carry Eliza up the banks of the Willamette River. They arrived in Portland with $2.75 to make a life with.

Ezra became wealthy farming hops, used to flavor malt liquors. He became famous and he and Eliza were received by Victoria, the Queen of England. He built an impressive Victorian mansion in Puyallup, Washington, the town they called home.

Ezra couldn't forget the Oregon Trail, so at 76, he traveled by ox-drawn wagon back over the Oregon Trail, this time in reverse. He traveled with his dog, his driver, and his two oxen on a trip that would take 11 months. As he traveled, he spoke of preserving the Oregon Trail. He met with President Theodore Roosevelt to ask for funding of the Oregon Trail Preservation Project.

In 1910, when he was 80 years old, he again went over the Oregon Trail to mark historical spots along the trail. This trip would take 2 years. In 1916, when he was 86, he traveled the trail again, this time to visit the Senate. He wanted the trail to be designated a military highway.

His last trip was made in an airplane, at the age of 94. This trip took 4 hours, compared to his original trip of 5 months. He met with President Calvin Coolidge and persuaded Congress to mint 6 million 50 cent Oregon Trail Memorial silver coins. 50 years after Ezra died, in 1978, the Oregon National Historic Trail was designated, thanks to the efforts of Ezra Meeker. [Wagner]

Voices from the past:

The "dead lay sometimes in rows of fifteen or more." **Ezra Meeker** *on how the number of graves on the trail resembled a battleground.*

"I longed to go back over the old Oregon Trail and mark it for all time for the children of the pioneers who blazed it, and for the world." **Ezra Meeker on speaking in schools about the importance of the Oregon Trail.** Wagner

Granite

G **ranite** is located way up in the Wallowa-Whitman National Forest in north eastern Baker County. It's a spectacularly beautiful, winding drive to get there. Granite's life began in 1862, when a local prospector and his mule became stuck in the mud while hauling whiskey. After getting the poor animal out, he noticed gold dust on his mule's hooves. [Weis]

By 1900, the town had a stable, post office, five saloons, three stores, a drug store, and two hotels. Granite also boasted a population of about 5000 people.

How to get to Granite:

Granite is 47 miles west of Baker City.

Southern Oregon

Cape Blanco State Park

Cape San Sebastian

S pectacular coastal scenery abounds at beautiful *Cape San Sebastian*, on the Oregon Coast. In 1603, this cape was visited by Sebastian Vicziano, a Spanish explorer who named the cape after the patron saint whose feast day was coming up.

How to get to Cape San Sebastian:

Cape San Sebastian is located on the Oregon Coast Highway near the southern coastal town of Gold Beach.

A word about sailor superstitions:

The rough, lonely life at sea was the perfect breeding ground for superstitions about doom and death. These are just a few of the many superstitions of the sea:

- Sailing on Friday was unlucky, because Jesus was crucified on a Friday.

- Red hair, crossed-eyes, or flat feet was bad luck.

- Flowers were said to bring bad luck, so they would be thrown overboard.

- Killing a seagull or dolphin would bring bad luck.

- Bare-breasted women were believed to calm the sea, which is why figureheads are often bare-breasted [Kitmacher]

McGowan,
Gardiner & the
Pioneer Cemetery

T he town of **McGowan** was founded around 1901. It was once the site of a large cannery. All that remains today is a quaint little church, which was locked when I visited.

Further along the coast, you will come to the tiny town of **Gardiner,** which began its life in 1850. A schooner named Bostonian wrecked on the Umpqua River Bar near this spot.

A merchant named Gardiner owned the schooner, so the town was named for him. Up until 1918, it was one of the busiest towns on the Oregon Coast.

Near Gardiner, stop by the **North Cove Pioneer Cemetery**, established in 1892. It lies right next to Hwy. 101, but in spite of the busy highway, the cemetery is a serene place.

How to get to McGowan, Gardiner, and North Cove Pioneer Cemetery:

McGowan, Gardiner, and North Cove Pioneer Cemetery are all located right along Hwy. 101 on the southern Oregon coast

Cape Blanco State Park

*C**ape Blanco State Park* contains the oldest lighthouse on the Oregon Coast. It was built in 1870, from locally-made brick. Additional building materials had to be shipped from San Francisco.

The *Hughes House* is also contained within the park. It was built in 1898 by Patrick and Jane Hughes.

The land surrounding the house reminded the Hughes family of their native Ireland. They eventually acquired over 2000 acres of land, established a dairy, and raised their own crops.

The house was unique for the time and isolated environment.

My favorite area of the house is the massive kitchen, complete with a huge cast-iron stove.

Many luxuries were added in-cluding acetylene lighting, indoor plumbing, and hot and cold run-ning water.

How to get to Cape Blanco State Park:

Cape Blanco State Park is near Port Orford, about 60 miles north of the Oregon/California border on Hwy. 101.

Jacksonville

The charming Southern Oregon town of *Jacksonville* began with the discovery of Gold in 1851. It soon became the biggest town in the Oregon Territory.

Today it contains many historic buildings and is a joy to walk around. Be sure to pick up the outstanding *Historic Landmark Walking Map* in the *Visitor's Center*.

After the gold discoveries became fewer and fewer, the town still remained vibrant as a major stopping point on a stagecoach route. In 1891 the railroad was built near Jacksonville, but didn't include Jacksonville, so the town began a slow decline.

As you walk around town, take your time because there is much to see including the oldest buildings, the *butcher shop*, *Love House*, and *St. Andrews Methodist-Episcopal Church*, all built in 1854.

Don't miss the *Jacksonville Cemetery*, established in 1860. It's one of the most picturesque cemeteries you will ever visit.

Also worth a visit is the 1880 *City Hall*, the oldest continuously used government building in Oregon

Other notable buildings include the ***Bella Union Saloon*** built in 1856, the 1891 ***Rogue River Valley Railway Depot***, the 1863 ***Beekman Bank***, which is the oldest bank in the Pacific Northwest, the 1911 ***Jackson County Jail***, and the 1908 ***Jacksonville School House***. City of Jacksonville, Oregon

How to get to Jacksonville:

Jacksonville is located in Southern Oregon, about 5 miles west of Medford.

Golden

The ghost town of ***Golden***, founded in 1890, is a mysterious place. In fact, it was featured on a popular paranormal investigation program because of the spiritual and ghostly activity there.

A coven of witches is said to inhabit the woods surrounding the town. I saw no one, but I can certainly imagine spiritual rites and rituals going on there.

Gold was found near the town in the 1850s, and structures began to spring up, including a ***church***, built in 1852. Eventually Golden would have two churches, but no saloons. [Weis]

The gold miners temporarily abandoned the town pursuing a gold strike in Idaho in 1860. When they returned to Golden, their claims had been usurped by 500 Chinese, who worked for ten cents a day and all of the rice they

could eat. In total, $1,500,000 in
gold was pulled out from around Golden.

As you walk the serene grounds of
Golden, don't miss the little white
schoolhouse.

The tiny *cemetery* contains just
a few graves, including the grave
of Marion Ellis, born in 1912,
died in 1992, a gold miner.

How to get to Golden:

Golden is located in Southern
Oregon off of I-5 by taking the Wolf Creek exit. The address is
3482 Coyote Creek Road.

Favorite Places to Camp

*F*ort Stevens is a massive state park, in a perfect location to tour Northwestern beaches and Astoria. The park has its own historic military installation and the wreck of the Peter Iredale. The campground has over 300 electrical sites, 6 tent sites 15 yurts, and 11 deluxe cabins. For information and reservations, contact *reserveamerica.com*

Clyde Holliday State Recreation Site is an excellent choice from which to explore the John Day Fossil Beds and other Central Oregon sites. The campground contains 31 electrical sites with water, on a first-come, first-served basis as of this writing. The park is beautiful, with a nice walking trail right alongside the river. For reservations, please visit *stateparks.oregon.gov*

Bullards Beach State Park is a huge, beautiful campground located on Hwy. 101 in Southern Oregon. The park has a paved walking trail to the beach and it's own historic lighthouse, built in 1899. The campground has over 200 campsites with hook-ups. For more information and reservations, contact ***reserveameric a.com***

Random Thoughts

What History Means to Me

F irst, let me start by sharing with you my opinion of what history isn't. History is not a collection of random dates, names, and places for you to memorize. History is not a dry and uninteresting class you have to pass to graduate.

I believe history is a tangible thing. You can actually *feel* history in the places you go, and the sights you see. I remember walking up to the Acropolis in Athens. I looked down at the well-worn marble steps and wondered about how many ancient philosophers had climbed these very steps, thousands of years ago.

You don't have to go far away to experience the *feeling* of history. If you are lucky enough to live in an old house, you may experience history in your own surroundings. You might say to yourself, *"If only these walls could talk."*

During my travels across the United States, I *felt* history in many, many places. If you travel across the country like I did, you will *feel* the wonderful history of our beautiful country for yourself, and you will never be the same. You will discover what it means to be an American.

Why I did it and why you can too:

I decided to travel across the country by car because I wanted to rediscover America. When I first set out to explore the history of our country, I wanted to find out why America is the greatest country on earth, and what it means to be an American.

The politics of these United States was frightening at the time. Our country was polarized, almost beyond repair. Whether it was Democrats or Republicans, Conservatives, or Liberals, everyone was fighting.

I wanted to rediscover the joy of being an American. I wanted to rediscover our rich history, our unique and wonderful people, our tapestry of multicultural heritage, and our rich natural resources. I thought a road trip by car across eleven western states was a good place to start.

I have a degree in Archaeology, and a passion for all things archaeological. I love history, with a side love of paleontology. It is these three passions that I set my trip agenda around. I set out to discover the archaeological sites, history, and paleontological world of our country.

As I travel and write my books, I get asked all the time, especially by women, "What is it like to travel by yourself? Aren't you scared?" The truth is, I believe everyone should do what I did. It's a wonderful way to discover our country, and to rediscover yourself. The truth is, I'm scared not to travel. Traveling allows you to get to know yourself, in ways not possible when sitting on the couch watching TV.

We tend to spend a lot of our lives tuning out the world and our place within it. When you travel, you are quite literally forced to deal with your own thoughts, emotions, and feelings. You can discover yourself while traveling. You can come to understand what makes you who you are, and how you can perhaps become a better person. Above all, traveling gives you mental clarity to figure out how to live with intent. It's a way to guide your life, not just wait for things to happen.

Travel Tips & Stuff
What You Need to Know

How to get started:

P lanning your trip should be one of the most exciting things about it. You want to be spontaneous, but it is also very wise to plan your route, so you can take full advantage of all the time and miles you will invest.

First, decide your passions. If you love airplanes, trains, or old vehicles, plan your trip around that. If you love gardens or architecture, seek that out as the focus of your trip.

Next, read and research areas of the country that will let you enjoy what you are interested in.

- Make a list by state and city or town, of what you want to see.

- Take your handy road atlas and locate the areas on the pages.

- Make a tentative route plan, so you have an idea of where you are going.

Travel tip: Avoid trying to plan your trip down to a schedule of days, hours, or minutes. On a road trip, it will be virtually impossible to know where you will be on any given day. If you adhere to a schedule, you are more likely to stress out, and less likely to actually enjoy yourself, which is the whole point.

What you need:

You need to bring along a sense of adventure and a curious mind. You need to ditch the idea of always being on a schedule, and live a little more spontaneously to thoroughly enjoy yourself. Things will happen as you travel, both good things and bad things, and you need to prepare your mind and your soul for day-to-day changes.

So much of our lives are planned out. Between growing up, going to school, finding a career, marriage, kids, or whatever, people have lost much of the ability to be spontaneous. But you must take spontaneity on the trip with you, because you may make detours along the way to see something really spectacular.

So, for the practical stuff you need:

A great vehicle-I have a Honda CRV which is fabulous. It's old, a 2004, fully paid for, and will go anywhere. I see humongous RVs on the road, towing a car behind, and all I can think of is, they can't go just anywhere. They are too big. Bad gas mileage, cumbersome to drive, slow, and not agile like my CRV. So, I encourage you, if you want to go car camping and be able to go on remote dirt roads, get an agile vehicle, and Hondas are great.

Travel tip: Don't be afraid to do some modifications to your vehicle. I took one of my back seats out. (after watching a YouTube video) I threw in a twin mattress, a bit of drapery, and some netting. I also put some of those little portable light switches on the inside. I jettisoned anything I hadn't used up to that point. Don't be afraid to get rid of unnecessary stuff.

An awesome camera that you know inside and out. I use a Nikon and it takes wonderful pictures. Don't skimp on a camera, and don't think a cellphone camera is all you need, because you want the best for your beautiful photos.

A hot plate warmer-this little item was indispensable. You need a converter for it so you can plug it in to the cigarette lighter. Place your food inside it, carton and all, and then plug it in. 30 minutes for thawed food, about an hour and a half for frozen food. Boom! You have a hot meal by the time you stop for the night!

Window shades-the best ones are magnetic so you just place them against your windows and they cling to them, obscuring the view inside your car.

Portable cooler with wheels-another indispensable item that works great and is easy to move around. I use those nifty blue frozen blocks in mine.

Portable air compressor-this little gem plugs into your cigarette lighter and will inflate your tires if you have a flat. Fortunately, I haven't had to use this yet.

Portable battery charger and power bank-mine comes with battery cables and the power bank, yet once inside the case, it is small enough to put in your glove compartment. This little item, unfortunately, I have had to use, and it saved me.

Portable generator-mine came with a small solar panel, so it can be charged with solar or electricity. It has a decent battery life and also doubles as a light for night-time.

All season clothing-you never know what different states will bring for weather, so take hot weather and cold weather clothes, and a fair amount of shoes appropriate for hiking, or walking, sandals, and slippers, which are nice at night. Also take along a pair of cheap rubber flip-flops to wear in the public showers you might go into.

Your own pillows-I like my own pillows, so I don't wake up with neck cramps, especially after sleeping in the car.

Sleeping bag and cozy blankets-you want to stay warm and layering is everything.

Warm hat, warm socks, and fuzzy jammies to keep you warm for cold nights sleeping in the car.

A great road atlas, and great guidebooks-get one that's easy to read, with great pictures. For a road atlas, just get one that is easy to read.

A word about photography:

Along with a great camera, you need to have a great eye. This is easier than it sounds once you have worked with your camera and are comfortable taking pictures with it. I am not a professional photographer, but I like my pictures and other people do too.

These are my tips for taking great pictures:

- Experiment with taking both horizontal and vertical shots.

- Don't always put the subject of the photo in the middle of the photograph.

- This one is important: pay attention to the foreground, and if possible, have something, a plant or whatever, in the foreground to help give the photo dimension and depth.

- This one is important too: turn around often to see the view you just came from. I do this quite often and some of my best pictures have resulted from when I turned around and took the shot.

You can also take a mental photo. Place an image in your mind that you can call upon later. Use all of your senses to see, hear, smell, and maybe even to taste, what is around you. You have the means to fully experience your surroundings, and that is very important to a traveler. When you take a mental photo, be sure to jot down quick little details about what you saw, heard, smelled, or tasted, so you can jog your memory later.

And last, but not least...don't be posing in front of everything, everywhere, to show that you actually went somewhere. Most people want to see themselves in your photo and be mentally transported there, but they can't if you are there already.

To camp or not to camp:

Car camping is great. I prefer it to sleeping on the cold, hard ground in a tent. I can lock the doors, put my window shades up and be cozy for the night.

That being said, for me there were some do's and don'ts about camp sites. Some people camp in a Walmart parking lot and feel safe. I do not. I believe that if you are in a busy area, you're more likely to be confronted by a nut job who may bother you. Nothing against Walmart.

Same goes for casino parking lots. Many people believe that if they are in a public place, there is less chance of someone bothering them. I don't share this belief. I believe you are safer parked out in the middle of nowhere in the dark. That same nut job who can find you in a parking lot is not about to go driving around on dirt roads to see if anyone is parked there. At least that's my belief. You may not share it, and that's fine. Park and camp wherever you feel safe.

I don't go for rest areas either because they have a track record of incidents happening to people in rest areas, especially women travelers.

So, where do I camp? In state or national campgrounds, wildlife sanctuaries, or off on a dirt road somewhere, usually out in the middle of nowhere.

There are definitely times when I stay in a motel. I use Hotels.com because I like their stay 10 nights, get 1 night free deal. So, I book a hotel or motel if:

- The weather is too hot or too cold, or too rainy

- I am in a city and plan to stay awhile

- I'm tired of camping, need a shower, or my body hurts

- I need to do laundry

A word about safety:

When you are a woman traveling alone, it's critical to keep a low profile. Don't tell people you are traveling alone, where you are staying, or any other personal information.

I don't go to bars or get drunk. I'm not preaching but you are on your own, in a city or town you've never been to, and you don't know anyone, so it's not the time to lose control of what you are doing. When you are in control, you are better able to decide which people you want to get to know better.

Travel tip: If you feel vulnerable traveling alone, that's OK. Vulnerability is part of passion, and traveling is a passionate thing to do. You can put one of those family stickers on your vehicle to indicate to others that you are not traveling alone, which can help you feel more secure.

Maintain your connections:

When you are traveling alone, there is a definite sense of disconnection. It feels almost like you are the only one in the world, traveling through space and time. That's why it's critical to keep your connections to loved ones active.

Be on Facebook while you are traveling. You may not have internet a lot of the time, or the internet will be poor. Consider paying to have your phone be a hotspot. It's a little bit of money per month, but it's worth it and has saved me from being without internet. I love the convenience of it, and you will too.

Plan your journey around visiting family members or friends you haven't seen for a long time, or people that are good friends. When you see people you know, it will ground you, so you can continue traveling.

Check in by phone with loved ones. They worry about you, and it's good for both of you to stay connected no matter where you are.

Consider traveling with a pet. I started my trip with my beloved 14-year-old sheltie named Sadie. She didn't make it to the end of the trip. I lost her to bladder cancer about four months in. My Sadie was special, and I will never forget my first traveling buddy.

It took me a solid year to decide on getting another dog. I poured over profiles of rescue dogs, looking for a little buddy I could take care of. Best Friends Animal Society in Kanab, Utah, had my perfect match. I now have Rosie, an 8 year-old sheltie that looks just like Sadie and has many of the same mannerisms. Life is good again.

I highly recommend Best Friends Animal Society if you are looking for a pet. They have 3000 acres and house up to 1600 animals at one time including dogs, cats, horses, pigs, and just about everything else. The dedicated people at Best Friends are wonderful both to you, and your potential pet.

Travel tip: One of the easiest and best ways I stay connected while traveling is to offer to take a photo for someone I don't know. Many couples, families, or singles would love to have more pictures of themselves traveling. It's an easy and quick way to have a connection with a fellow traveler, and it's good manners too.

Practical matters:

You need to have an address to send your mail to. Keep in touch with whomever is nice enough to do this for you.

You will also need to come back occasionally to register your car, vote, go to doctor visits, and take care of any other business. You can't leave it all behind, as tempting as that may be.

Bad things that happened:

Remember when I said you need to take spontaneity with you on your trip? Well, there were many times when I used my spontaneity skillset.

The government shutdown happened smack dab in the middle of my travels. That meant that all of the National Monuments were closed. I did a lot of driving and circling around.

I also did a lot of circling around trying to avoid natural disasters. I traveled through Paradise, California shortly before a massive fire happened there. I tried to travel through the area again but was pushed out by massive flooding. My latest event was camping in Canyonville, Oregon and waking up to flames creeping down the hillside. That was day one of the Canyonville fire.

Besides being driven out by natural disasters, sometimes I was driven out by rude people. Many times it was centered around my furry traveling companion. I believe there are really only two types of people, those who love animals and those who don't. When people see me walking my beautiful, sweet, elderly dog, they either come up and pet her, or they say something harsh.

One incident was a woman, a total stranger, who came up to me smiling down at Sadie and asked how old she was. I replied, "She is 13 and a half years old." The woman replied very curtly "She needs to be put down." Sadie was walking around, alert, and happy, and yet this woman wanted me to end her life because she was old.

Speaking of animals, several times I came very close to driving into an animal on the road. I can't stress enough how many times this will happen to you, and all I can say is, be alert at all times while you are driving. When you travel a lot of miles, you will get tired, so stop and smell the roses, and try not to drive at night.

Good things that happened:

One of the sheer joys of taking a road trip is the unpredictability of it. You never know what you will see. I am originally from Oregon, and bears are not a common sight. So, while driving high up in the Blue Mountains, I looked over and saw a bear! So exciting! He didn't stay for long, kind of shy, but so cute. I love animals, so to see the rich and wonderful amount of wildlife in our country gladdened my heart.

I met many great people on my trip, from all walks of life. They were a walking, talking advertisement for our beautiful country. I smiled at them, and they smiled back. We are all Americans, and we are all part of the human race. When you meet people across the country, you realize just how important it is to get to know your fellow citizens, and learn more about how they view the world and our country.

I have to give a special shout-out to the many dedicated people, often volunteers, who staff our state and national parks and monuments. They work tirelessly to ensure the health of our natural resources, and help travelers enjoy their visit. The same is true of the many people who staff the museums in small towns and large cities. They enjoy history, like I do, and it shows in their smiles.

Along with wonderful people, I have seen an America that is spectacularly beautiful, with open prairies, majestic mountains, and crystal clear rivers. I have seen a small fraction of the history of our country. I have seen the memorials to the brave people who shaped our country. I have fallen in love with America in a way that was not possible sitting in my living room. People ask me, "would I do it again?" The answer comes easily, "Yes, in a heartbeat."

Bibliography and Further Reading

Cape Blanco Heritage Society, *Historic Hughes House and Ranch*

Clatsop County Historical Society, *Flavel House Museum*

Davis, Jefferson and Janine, *A Haunted Tour Guide to the Pacific Northwest*, Norsemen Ventures, 2010.

Enss, Chris. *Tales behind the Tombstones*. Morris Pub., 2007.

Enss, Chris. *The Doctor Wore Petticoats: Women Physicians of the Old West*. TwoDot, 2006.

Finch, etc. al.., Jackie. *Eyewitness Travel USA*. DK Publishing, 2017.

Glassman, Steve. *It Happened on the Santa Fe Trail*. Twodot, 2008.

Golden History Park Walking Guide, Golden History

Hill, William E. *The Oregon Trail, Yesterday and Today: a Brief History and Pictorial Journey along the Wagon Tracks of Pioneers*. Caxton Press, 2014.

Hot Lake Springs , Hot Lake Springs

Independence Loop Trail Guide, Wallowa Whitman National Forest

Jacksonville Historic Landmark Walking Map, City of Jacksonville Oregon

Johnson, Mary E. Benson. *Reminiscences of Oregon Pioneers*. East Oregonian Pub. Co., 1937.

Jones, Landon Y. *The Essential Lewis and Clark*. HarperCollins Publishers, 2000.

Kitmacher, Ira Wesley, *Haunted Graveyard of the Pacific*, History Press, 2021.

Lewis and Clark National and State Historical Parks, National Park Service

Oregon City Loop Guide, Wallowa Whitman National Forest

Oregon State Parks, *Fort Yamhill State Heritage Area*

Peck, David J. *Or Perish in the Attempt: The Hardship and Medicine of the Lewis and Clark Expedition*. The History Press, 2002.

Stark, Peter. *Astoria: John Jacob Astor and Thomas Jefferson's Lost Pacific Empire: a Story of Wealth, Ambition, and Survival*. Harper Collins, 2014.

Wagner, Tricia Martineau. *It Happened on the Oregon Trail: Remarkable Events That Shaped History*. GPP, 2014.

Weeks, Andy. *Haunted Oregon: Ghosts and Strange Phenomena of the Beaver State*. Stackpole Books, 2014.

Weis, Norm. *Ghost Towns of the Northwest*. Caxton Printers, 2002.

Index

Referenced by Sections

D

About the Author

Julie Bettendorf is a world traveler with a degree in archaeology and a background in history. She has traveled extensively throughout Egypt, Central America, South America, Europe, and the United Kingdom, visiting archaeological and historical sites all along the way.

Currently, Julie is traveling around the US visiting ghost towns, ancient rock art sites, and archaeological wonders as part of research for her ongoing historical travel series entitled Wandering Woman. Wandering Woman is a set of state-by-state guides, full of photographs, historical anecdotes, and unique tips to help other women travel and explore solo across the US by car. Julie enjoys writing freelance blogs, traveling frequently with her two adult children, and hiking outdoors with her faithful dog companion Rosie.

Also by Julie Bettendorf

Wandering Woman: Oregon is the fifth book in the *Wandering Woman Travel Series*. The first four books *Wandering Woman: Montana*, *Wandering Woman: Utah*, *Wandering Woman: Nevada*, and *Wandering Woman: Colorado* are available in ebook and paperback.

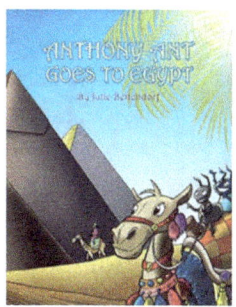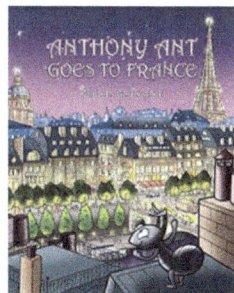

Julie has published two children's books in an ongoing, beautifully illustrated travel series entitled ***Anthony Ant Goes to France*** and ***Anthony Ant Goes to Egypt.***

She has also published a work of historical fiction entitled ***Luxor: Book of Past Lives*** which has recently been released as an audiobook, read by renowned narrator Barry Shannon.

www.ingramcontent.com/pod-product-compliance
Lightning Source LLC
Chambersburg PA
CBHW070709130626
46553CB00005B/1902